Proverbs 3:5-6

Am I Making Sense?

Making Sense of Fasting & Praying

by
Pastor Gusta Booker

Orman Press
Lithonia, Georgia

Making Sense of Fasting and Praying

by
Gusta Booker

ISBN: 1-891773-54-2

Scripture quotations are taken from THE HOLY BIBLE, *King James Version.*

Printed in the United States of America

10 9 8 7 6 5 4 3 2 1

Orman Press, Inc.
Lithonia, Georgia

Acknowledgements

I dedicate this book to my late father, Rev. Gusta Booker, Sr., and mother, Gussie Booker, who taught me principles by which I continue to live daily.

Words cannot express my gratitude for the superior spiritual support I have received from my wife, Theola, for over forty years.

Thanks to my children, Ronald, who is my co-pastor; Gusta III who keeps me on my toes with his questions; and my daughter, Alita, who I am working tirelessly to unspoil.

Thanks to every member of Greater St. Matthew Church who has listened to my messages for over thirty-five years and continued to live victoriously from them.

Special thanks to our Media Ministry for diligently working to professionally record every sermon that is preached.

Table of Contents

Introduction

Why Fast and Pray? 1

Chapter One

Words to the Wise on Fasting and Praying 5

Chapter Two

The Church That Fasts and Prays 9

Chapter Three

Facing Adversaries Through Fasting and Praying 19

Chapter Four

Fasting and Praying to Break the Yoke of Depression 27

Chapter Five

Fasting and Praying for Patience 39

About the Author 57

Why Fast and Pray?

I f you have never fasted and prayed before, the first thing you probably want to know is: Why should I?

The answer to that question is simple: Because your body is the temple of God. That means that in order for God to do His perfect work, some things must come out of the temple so He can have a committed spirit. Just think about all the things we put into our bodies and how they affect us physically. When you give your body a rest from food, you let nature take its course.

There are references to fasting and praying throughout the Bible. Moses fasted before he received the Ten Commandments. Look at Deuteronomy 9:9, which says:

> *When I was gone up into the mount to receive the tables of stone, even the tables of the covenant which the Lord made with you, then I abode in the mount forty days and forty nights, I neither did eat bread nor drink water.*

As a young man growing up in the small town of Columbus, Texas, I learned about the importance of fasting and praying at an early age. I was the youngest of nine children born to the late Rev. Gusta Booker, Sr., and the late Mrs. Gussie Booker. My parents taught us all about fasting and how God would give us spiritual and physical strength, if we fasted and prayed on a regular basis.

I admit that when I was younger, it was hard for me to appreciate fasting and praying. Like most teenagers, I was very conscious of peer pressure, and none of my friends did it. I also loved to eat, just as I do now, and wasn't happy about missing any meals.

My mother was a marvelous cook who believed in preparing stick-to-your-rib meals. I can still taste her cooking now—homemade cornbread, delicious mustard greens, savory smothered steak, sweet candied yams, and a rich, buttery pound cake that she baked especially for me. She and my father knew that missing a meal or two was a small price to pay for what fasting and praying offered—a renewed sense of God's presence and love for us.

It was not until I enrolled in Texas Southern University and met my wife-to-be, Theola, that I really began to take fasting and praying seriously. Theola had a lot of Christian principles that helped pull me out of the wilderness, including a strong belief in fasting and praying. My commitment grew as we fasted and prayed together while dating. That was thirty-five years ago. Today, we still fast and pray, and we encourage our family, friends, and church members at Greater St. Matthew to join us.

I now fast from one to three days a week on a regular basis. I advise members of my church to start by fasting and praying each Wednesday from 6 a.m. to 6 p.m. Some of our more experienced saints fast two or three days each week, but I recommend a happy medium so other members will not be easily frustrated.

I can tell you from my personal experiences that once you successfully complete a fast, you feel wonderful and victorious. It's like taking a test and passing, or playing a game and winning. In actuality, you have won a victory for God.

I pray that *Making Sense of Fasting and Praying* will help you become victorious as well. It is the first book in a series designed to help Christians gain a clearer understanding of biblical principles, and how to apply them to everyday life. If you're wondering about the series title, it comes from a question I always ask during my sermons: Am I Making Sense? I certainly hope I am. God bless you and keep you.

Yours in Christ,
Pastor Gusta Booker

CHAPTER ONE

Words to the Wise on Fasting and Praying

Fasting and praying begins with a mindset and a plan. Your plan should include what you will do before, during, and after your fast. It is important that you properly prepare before you begin fasting and praying so God may perform His complete work in you. Here are some tips to help you prepare for your fast.

- **Know why you are fasting and praying.** Do you need help in overcoming sin? Are you seeking solutions to certain problems? Do you desire more power in your prayers? Whatever the reason, ask God for guidance to make sure you are on the right track. And remember this is not a diet so you are not fasting and praying to lose weight. Spend your time communicating with God, not jumping on and off the bathroom scales.
- **Prepare yourself physically.** Consult with your doctor before beginning a fast, especially

if you have health problems or take prescription medication. Once you get the go-ahead, do not make the mistake of "tanking up" by stuffing yourself with food. Instead, a few days beforehand, start preparing your body the right way by eating smaller meals, more raw fruits and vegetables, and avoiding foods that are high in fat, salt, and sugar.

- **Nourish yourself spiritually.** Fasting is a denial or abstinence until a certain breakthrough has come in your life. Fasting also involves prayer and repentance, which is why you must spend time alone with God. Develop a schedule in which you read and meditate on His word. Pray, pray, and pray some more. Prayer builds a hedge around you, and you will need it to fight the devil. Satan will attack you when you are at your weakest. He will try to destroy your purpose by making you think about food. Work with God so the devil won't succeed.

- **Do not deprive your body of nutrients.** There are different types of fasts, but I prefer a juice fast, which gives your body the nutrients it needs and reduces hunger pains. You can make your own fresh-squeezed fruit or vegetable juices, or buy juices that have no added sugar or other additives. Some good choices are apple, pear, grape, papaya, watermelon, carrot, celery, or leafy green vegetable juices. If you like orange or tomato juices, dilute them with water because of their high acid content. Avoid drinks with caffeine, such as coffee, tea, or cola.

- **Drink plenty of water.** Even on a juice fast, you should still drink plenty of water. It will help you feel full while preventing dehydration. In general, drinking water is one of the best things you can do for your body. Increased water consumption has been shown to help relieve migraine headaches, high cholesterol, rheumatoid arthritis pain, allergies, and high blood pressure. Water also flushes out toxins, helps eliminate heartburn, and can even make your skin look younger and softer. Once your fast ends, gradually return to solid food by eating small, healthy snacks, such as fresh fruit, vegetable salads, or plain baked potatoes.

- **Look your best.** The whole world doesn't have to know that you are fasting and praying. It's between you and God. Matthew 6:16 says, *"Moreover when ye fast, be not as the hypocrites of a sad countenance: for they disfigure their faces, that they may appear unto men to fast."* In other words, don't be like the hypocrites, who look disheveled so people will admire them for fasting. Verse 17 says, *"But thou when thou fasteth, anoint thine head and wash thy face."* That means you should also comb your hair and wash your face.

- **Rely on the strength of the Holy Spirit.** When you fast, you deny yourself of the *natural* so God can come in and add a little *super* to it. That's what we call *supernatural.* Think of Clark Kent, who without his cape, acts like any other man. He wears bifocals; he's always missing assignments at the newspaper; and he's late for everything. The man Clark Kent just can't seem to do anything right, but when he goes into a telephone booth and takes off his suit, he turns into Superman. You can't be a Superman without having the supernatural in your body.

CHAPTER TWO

The Church That Fasts and Prays

One of the many things I have learned during my years in the ministry is that the church that fasts and prays can do powerful things through our Lord and Savior Jesus Christ. The Bible talks about unity, power, and strength in numbers. Matthew 18:20 says, "For where two or three are gathered together in my name, there am I in the midst of them."

There have been many times when fasting and praying have taken our church to new heights. For example, when we needed funding to build our second location in Southwest Houston, the church fasted and prayed, and we received the financial help we needed. When we needed to take our television ministry to another level, we achieved it through fasting and prayer.

One of the numerous references to fasting and praying in the Bible, is found in Matthew 17:14–18. Jesus had led Peter, James, and John up a high mountain. A huge crowd was waiting when they arrived at the foot of the mountain. A man knelt before Jesus and said:

> *Lord, have mercy on my son: for he is a lunatic, and sore vexed: for ofttimes he falleth into the fire, and oft into the water. And I brought him to thy disciples, and they could not cure him. Then Jesus answered and said, O faithless and perverse generation, how long shall I be with you? How long shall I suffer you? bring him hither to me. And Jesus rebuked the devil; and he departed out of him: and the child was cured from that very hour (Matthew 17:15–18).*

Verses 19–20 tell us that after the child was cured, the disciples approached Jesus in private and said:

> *Why could not we cast him out? And Jesus said unto them, Because of your unbelief: for verily I say unto you, if ye have faith as a grain of mustard seed, ye shall say unto this mountain, Remove hence to yonder place; and it shall remove; and nothing shall be impossible unto you.*

Listen to what Jesus said next, in verse 21: *"Howbeit this kind goeth not out but by prayer and fasting."* In other words, Jesus was telling the disciples that kind of demon would not leave unless they fasted and prayed.

Fasting and praying is a powerful weapon indeed. It can heal us spiritually, physically, emotionally, financially—all kinds of ways. We are new creatures in

Christ, new converts, and one of the most meaningful things we can do in our Christian life is to fast. But you cannot fast without praying. If you're not going to pray, then don't fast.

By fasting, you will be following the example of other people in the Bible. When Hannah prayed and asked the Lord to give her a boy child, she refused to eat at that time (I Samuel 1:5–11). Not only that, but we also see that David fasted (II Samuel 12:16), and Paul fasted following his conversion on the Damascus road (Acts 9:1–9). You will find another reference to Jesus and fasting in Matthew 4. It is one of the best known Bible stories, and tells us that Jesus fasted in the wilderness for forty days and forty nights. When temptation came, He was able to resist the devil because He was spiritually prepared for the battle. You, too, can ward off Satan by fasting and praying.

THE BATTLE IS THE LORD'S

In my role as a church leader, I am often expected to have all the answers. I don't, of course; no man does. That is one reason why I am inspired by the story of King Jehoshaphat in the Old Testament (II Chronicles 20). He looked to the Lord for help when he didn't know the answer to a monumental problem, and he recognized the power of fasting and praying.

I have had my own Jehoshaphat experiences. I remember when Theola and I bought our first house in Southeast Houston on Jutland Road, the house where the first Greater St. Matthew Church services were held. We started with eight members, and we often tell the story of how on Sunday mornings, the choir marched from the bedroom into the living room, which served as our sanctuary. We kept our eyes on the Lord from the very beginning. We still do, and looking to the Lord during fasting and praying has been one of our guiding principles.

If you read the twentieth chapter of II Chronicles, you will see a group of armies about to attack Jehoshaphat, the King of Judah. Verses 1–3 reads:

> *It came to pass after this also, that the children of Moab, and the children of Ammon, and with them other beside the Ammonites, came against Jehoshaphat to battle. Then there came some that told Jehoshaphat, saying, There cometh a great multitude against thee from beyond the sea on this side of Syria; and, behold, they be in Hazazon-tamar, which is En-gedi. And Jehoshaphat feared, and set himself to seek the Lord, and proclaimed a fast throughout all Judah.*

Let's take a closer look at the last verse, which tells us some important things. First, the king was obviously afraid. We all know what a powerful emotion fear can be. The tragic events of September 11, 2001 showed us that one of the terrorists' main objectives was to make Americans afraid. If you aren't careful, fear can overtake you. Fear will keep you from getting on an airplane again. Fear will keep you from going into tall buildings. Fear will keep you awake at night.

But fear doesn't have to overwhelm you, if you do what Jehoshaphat did next: he set himself to seek the Lord. Brothers and sisters, we all need to get closer to the Lord. Start reading your Bible and stop letting dust gather on it like an old piece of furniture. Start going to church and stop letting the devil keep you under the covers on Sunday mornings. Sooner or later, you will have to depend on God. That's what Jehoshaphat did. He knew this was a big one and that he couldn't do it alone so he told the people of Judah, "Let's fast."

What happened after that? Walk with me through Chapter 20, starting at verse 4:

> *And Judah gathered themselves together, to ask help of the Lord: even out of all the cities of Judah they came to seek the Lord. And Jehoshaphat stood in the congregation of Judah and Jerusalem, in the house of the Lord, before the new court, And said, O Lord God of our fathers, are not thou God in heaven? and rulest not thou over all the kingdoms of the heathen? and in thine hand is there not power and might, so that none is able to withstand thee? (II Chronicles 20:4-6).*

Jehoshaphat was telling the Lord that he knew He was almighty. Let me tell you, it's good to brag on God. Tell Him, "Lord, You're awesome. Lord, You're somebody. Lord, I know that what I'm trying to ask you for is already done." Am I making sense?

HE CAN HANDLE IT

In II Chronicles 20:7 and 10, Jehoshaphat remembered what God had done in the past by saying:

> *Are not thou our God, who didst drive out the inhabitants of this land before thy people Israel, and gavest it to the seed of Abraham they friend forever? And now, behold, the children of Ammon and Moab and mount Seir, whom thou wouldest not let Israel invade, when they came out of the land of Egypt, but they turned from them, and destroyed them not.*

Jehoshaphat was saying, "Lord, aren't you the same God who brought us out of Egypt and gave us this land?"

In verses 11–12, he tells the Lord, "They're coming to take charge of what you have given us. Lord, where are You? We can't handle them God."

Well, guess what? There are many times when we can't handle our problems either. But the Lord can. I don't care if you know the Bible from Genesis to Revelations backward, you still need the Lord. You may be saying, "But Pastor Booker, I do fast and pray." If for some reason, you still don't get an answer after you have fasted and prayed, then check to make sure your eyes were truly on God.

In II Chronicles 20:15, we see that all of Judah stood before the Lord, and the Spirit of the Lord arrived in the midst of the congregation:

> *And he said, Hearken ye, all Judah, and ye inhabitants of Jerusalem, and thou king Jehoshaphat, Thus saith the Lord unto you, Be not afraid nor dismayed by reason of this great multitude; for the battle is not yours, but God's.*

In other words, God said, "Now wait a minute, Jehoshaphat. Yes, I'm going to talk to you. Number one, stop shaking! And don't be afraid or dismayed by what's going to happen to you. Do you know why? Because you can't fight this battle. This battle is not yours, Jehoshaphat. It's mine."

We can't fight our personal battles either, because the battles aren't ours. The battle is the Lord's. If we take our hands out of it, God can do His work. He doesn't need our assistance.

I remember all the times our church was faced with problems and we didn't know the answer. I called for a church-wide fast. We got down on our knees and prayed. There has never been a time that God didn't bring us out of whatever we were going through.

God certainly delivered Jehoshaphat from his problem. The next morning, the people of Judah and Jerusalem rose early and went into the wilderness to meet the armies that were coming to attack them. A large choir marched in front and began giving a concert right in the middle of the battlefield. As they sang, the Moabites and the Ammonites fought against the Edomites. After they killed the Edomites, they began to kill each other.

Do you see what happens when you get your hands out of it? God will make your enemies fight each other. You don't have to shoot a bullet; just sing a song. Everybody ought to have a song. Everybody ought to know how to call on God. When the devil hears you singing, he will flee.

DOES YOUR CHURCH NEED A BREAKTHROUGH?

Here are a few more thoughts to help the church fast and pray:

- Fasting confirms what Jesus said in Matthew 4:4 when he told the devil: *"Man shall not live by bread alone, but every word that proceeds out of the mouth of God."* Fasting is important, and it's not just for the preacher, the choir, the deacons, and the ushers. It's for everybody.
- Fasting increases a church's corporate faith.

- Fasting brings about a stronger response to God's Word.
- A church that fasts will experience a stronger fellowship between brothers and sisters.

CHAPTER THREE

Facing Adversaries Through Fasting and Praying

A n adversary is an enemy or an opposing force. Adversaries come in all shapes, forms, and fashions. They are all around us. Drug and alcohol abuse, lust, lying, laziness, cheating, greed—are all adversaries. Food can be an adversary if you eat too much and/or eat the wrong things. Even work can be an adversary if it consumes too much of your life. The four-star general of adversaries is Satan. He has many devices for luring us into his web of evil, including all of the above.

One way to decipher and discern the devil's tricks is through fasting and praying. When we fast and pray, we connect with God, and God gives us strength to face our adversaries. God will let you know everything is going to be alright. All you have to do is hang in there and He will give you strength. If you have any doubts about God's power and glory, just look at Psalm 27:1–3:

The Lord is my light and my salvation; whom shall I fear? the Lord is the strength of my life; of whom shall I be afraid? When the wicked, even mine enemies and my foes, came upon me to eat up my flesh, they stumbled and fell. Though an host should encamp against me, my heart shall not fear: though war should rise against me, in this will I be confident.

Did you hear what David said? He said that when his foes attacked him, they would stumble and fall. Your foes will fall too, because fasting and praying gives you an edge.

There is a story about two lumberjacks who made their living cutting down trees. One of them was a young man with bulging muscles and the strength of an ox. The other was an older man who wasn't so strong anymore. One day, they had a contest to see which one of them could cut down the most trees. They started cutting down trees early that morning, and kept going until three o'clock that afternoon. When the contest was over, the officials counted the trees. Everyone was surprised to see that the old man had cut down twice as many as the young man. The young man who was dead tired and dripping with sweat couldn't understand what happened. During the contest, he kept chopping the whole time, but the old man kept taking breaks and sitting down. So he asked the old man, "How did you manage to win the contest?" The old man explained, "Every time I stopped to sit down, I sharpened my axe. A sharp axe cuts better and faster than a dull one, and that's how I beat you."

My point is: if you stop, fast, and pray, it will sharpen your axe. There are things in our lives that cannot be cut down with a dull axe.

If you look in the Old Testament in the Book of Esther, you will find a good example of how fasting and praying can help you defeat your adversaries. The gist of the story is in Chapter 4, verses 15–17:

> *Then Esther bade them return Mordecai this answer, Go, gather together all the Jews that are present in Shushan, and fast ye for me, and neither eat nor drink three days, night or day: I also and my maidens will fast likewise; and so will I go in unto the king, which is not according to the law: and if I perish, I perish. So Mordecai went his way, and did according to all Esther had commanded him.*

Esther told Mordecai and all of the Jewish people to fast, and then whatever happened, so be it. If she perished, she perished.

Esther was a beautiful Hebrew woman who lived in Persia. The king of Persia, Ahasuerus, had a lot of parties and celebrations. Princes from India, Arabia and Ethiopia attended his lavish celebrations. They walked on streets made of marble, reclined on couches made of gold and silver, and drank an abundance of wine from gold cups.

During one of his celebrations, the king had too much to drink, and summoned his queen, Vashti, to come and show off her royal beauty. She refused. The king became angry and decided that Vashti would no longer be his wife as punishment for her disobedience. After Vashti was stripped of her title, fair, young virgins were brought before the king so he could pick a new wife. Esther was part of that group, and God saw fit that Esther would be the chosen one. The king picked Esther to be the new queen.

There was a man on the king's staff, Haman, who had a vendetta against the Jews because of Mordecai, Esther's cousin. Mordecai would not bow down to Haman, so Haman plotted to have Mordecai and all the Jews killed. Mordecai appealed to Esther to help by going to the king on behalf of her people.

Now Esther loved her people and was devastated when she discovered there was a decree that all the Hebrews be killed. However, there was a law that anyone going to the king without being summoned would be killed, even if she were his wife. Mordecai reminded Esther, *"Who knoweth whether thou art come to the kingdom for such a time as this?" (Esther 4:14).* So she decided to go to the king and ask him to spare the Jews. That is when Esther told Mordecai to gather all the Jews and fast for three days.

In Chapter 5, we see that on the third day, Esther put on her royal garments and entered the inner court of the palace, which was across from the king's hall. Verse 2 says:

> *And it was so, when the king saw Esther the queen standing in the court, that she obtained favor in his sight: and the king held out to Esther the golden scepter that was in his hand. So Esther drew near, and touched the top of the scepter.*

That verse shows us that when we stand for God, God can change people's hearts through our fasting and praying.

The king then spoke kindly to Esther and asked her what she wanted. Esther was still too frightened to tell him so she answered, *"If it seem good unto the king, let the king and Haman come this day unto the banquet that I have prepared for him"* (Esther 5:4). Later at the banquet, the king asked Esther again what she wanted. Once again, she postponed telling him.

Meanwhile, Haman went home a happy man because he had been invited to the banquet by the queen. But on his way out of the gate, his joy vanished when he saw that Mordecai would not bow down to him. Haman's wife and friends saw how this disturbed him so they suggested he build a gallows to hang Mordecai.

There was another banquet in Esther 7. The king asked Esther again what she wanted, and assured her that he would grant her request. Esther asked the king to spare her life and the lives of her people. She told the king that her people had been sold to those who would kill, slaughter, and annihilate them. The king was shocked and asked who would do such a thing. *"And Esther said, 'The adversary and enemy is this wicked Haman.' Then Haman was afraid before the king and the queen" (Esther 7:6).*

Haman had every right to be afraid. His plotting and scheming reminds me of an old song the quartets used to sing: "When you dig one ditch, you better dig two." He was hanged on the gallows he had built for Mordecai, and Esther saved the Hebrew people.

You can overcome your adversaries and enemies when you fast and pray. Nothing is too hard for God. He can make it work. I know there have been times when my car stopped running, and I was ready to sell it. But when I took it to the mechanic, the problem turned out to be one little wire. You should not give up too soon either, even if your life has gone awry. Invite God in through fasting and praying, and watch Him move.

Remember what it says in Psalm 27:1, *"The Lord is my light and my salvation."* Let's examine the light for a moment in terms of light from a fire. Sometimes when we are going through a lot of trouble, we say, "I'm going through the fire." But a fire doesn't just burn; a fire can light your path or keep you warm. When the Lord is your Light, He can make your disaster a blessing.

Just like Esther approaching her king, we have a King in Jesus Christ, and He will take care of us. God is standing near and He knows how much we can bear. One writer said that God has His eyes on the thermometer and His hand on the thermostat. When it gets a little too hot, He turns it down.

DO YOU NEED A BREAKTHROUGH?

If you are facing adversaries in your life and are in need of a personal breakthrough, then perhaps these words of advice will help you as you fast and pray:

- Know that the devil will come after you while you are fasting so do not let him tempt you. If you feel like you are succumbing to the flesh, get out of the kitchen and go outside for some fresh air and a short walk. Instead of eating, talk with God and commune with nature. And don't forget to drink water or juice throughout the day. It will help ease your hunger pains.

- If you have tried fasting before and failed, I admonish you to not give up. Even if you only make it through half a day, try again. The next time, you might make it through a whole day, then two days, and then three days. Each victory, no matter how small, will bring you one step closer to your goal. Just don't go backward; go forward.

- Do not get so caught up in fasting that you neglect prayer. Fasting and praying go hand and hand. You should not fast, if you are not going to pray. Also, there is general prayer and specific prayer. Sometimes you need to get away from the general and be specific. Specific prayer develops your faith. Faith is like muscle. The more you use it, the stronger it becomes.

- I have been preaching for a long time, and I have seen the Lord do much. What He has done for me, He can do for you. You might not think you are worthy, but He looks beyond your faults. If there is a problem and you need a breakthrough, when you have tried everything, maybe the solution you are looking for will come through fasting and praying.

CHAPTER FOUR

Fasting and Praying to Break the Yoke of Depression

D epression is something people do not like to talk about. We keep it hush-hush because the last thing we want is for someone to think that we are mentally unstable. But depression is a serious problem, and one way to combat the problem is by turning it over to God.

We all get the blues at one time or another. It is a normal reaction to everyday life. However, if your feeling of sadness is intense or lasts for long periods of time, you should get professional help right away. According to the National Mental Health Association, you should see your doctor or a qualified mental health professional if you experience five or more of the following symptoms for longer than two weeks or if the symptoms are severe enough to interfere with your daily routine:

- Restlessness or irritability
- Fatigue or loss of energy
- Sleeping too little or too much

- Reduced appetite and weight loss or increased appetite and weight gain
- Loss of interest or pleasure in activities you once enjoyed
- Difficulty concentrating, remembering, or making decisions
- Thoughts of death or suicide

If you only experience the blues occasionally and your doctor says it is okay, by all means consider fasting and praying to break the yoke of depression.

Am I making sense?

Let's walk through the Book of Kings and see how God helped Elijah break the yoke of depression. Elijah was a great prophet. He was known for his miracles and his opposition to the worship of the pagan god, Baal. But he was also in mental turmoil. Elijah began to withdraw and run away from his problems. Running away from our problems is not the answer. We have to face them.

One of the great Bible stories tells of Elijah standing alone at Mount Carmel. It all started when he challenged Ahab, the wicked king of Israel and the husband of Jezebel, to a showdown. Israel had begun to worship idols because of Queen Jezebel, and Elijah just got tired of it. So Elijah told Ahab to bring all of the people of Israel to Mount Carmel with four hundred fifty prophets of Baal and four hundred prophets of Asherah. First Kings 18:21 says:

> *And Elijah came unto all the people, and said, How long halt ye between two opinions? if the Lord be God, follow him: but if Baal, then follow him. And the people answered him not a word.*

Elijah explained that they were going to build altars, and the God that answered by fire would be the God they would serve. The Scripture says he let the prophets of Baal try to start the fire first. The followers of Baal began to worship, pray, and scream, but no fire came. They began to cut themselves and bleed, but still there was no fire. Elijah made fun of them and said in so many words, "Maybe your god can't hear you. Scream a little louder." When you serve idol gods, they cannot hear you. They may have ears, but they cannot hear your pleas.

After it became apparent that the heathens' god did not have the power to start a fire, Elijah told the people who were watching this spectacle, *"Come near unto me"(I Kings 18:30)*. He took twelve stones and built an altar in the name of the Lord. He even had the people pour water on the altar several times so no one could say he used trickery. Then, Elijah began to cry out to God. The Lord answered Elijah with fire, and all of Baal's worshippers were killed.

This was a great victory for Elijah, but it wasn't the end of the story. Sometimes in life, defeat follows victory. Isn't it funny how just when you think you've got it made, something else comes up? Keep in mind that when you have a success, you become a prime candidate for Satan's attack. I remember when our church was about to go into our second location on South Main in Houston. I told the congregation, "We had better take prayer over there because after every victory, the devil starts lurking to see how he can tear you down."

You may have just gotten a promotion on your job, but keep praying. You may have a new house, but keep praying. You may have met the man or woman of your dreams, but keep praying. It's okay to celebrate, but you have to keep praying. I can't stress it enough. The devil lurks after every victory.

First Kings 19:1–3 describes what happened to Elijah after his triumph on Mount Carmel:

> *And Ahab told Jezebel all that Elijah had done, and withal how he had slain all the prophets with the sword. Then Jezebel sent a messenger unto Elijah, saying, So let the gods do to me, and more also, if I make not thy life as the life of one of them by tomorrow about this time. And when he saw that, he arose, and went for his life, and came to Beersheba, which belongeth to Judah, and left his servant there.*

When Jezebel found out what Elijah had done and how he had killed the prophets of Baal, she wanted revenge. She promised to kill Elijah by the same time on the next day. Elijah got scared and fled for his life. Now, he had just won a battle in which God started fire with wet wood (and everyone knows you can't start a fire with wet wood). Yet, Elijah was running from Jezebel.

We see Elijah's depression in I Kings 19:4:

> *But he himself went a day's journey into the wilderness, and came and sat down under a juniper tree: and he requested for himself that he might die; and said, It is enough; now, O Lord, take away my life; for I am not better than my fathers.*

Elijah was so depressed that he told the Lord he wanted to die right then and there. I am sure he didn't mean it. When we are down and out, we often say things we don't mean. How do I know Elijah didn't really want to die? Because he was running for his life. If he had wanted to die, Jezebel would have taken his life for him. All he had to do was stay put and she would have had him killed.

REST, SWEET REST

In I Kings 19:5, we see that the first thing Elijah needed to do was rest. *"And as he lay and slept under a juniper tree, behold, then an angel touched him, and said unto him, Arise and eat."* Sometimes we get down and out because we are burning the candle on both ends. When that happens, we need sleep. When we settle down, God starts dealing with our bodies.

We also see that the angel told Elijah to *"Arise and eat."* When Elijah looked, he saw a cake baked on the coals and a cruse of water at his head. Now that wasn't a pineapple upside down cake or a German chocolate cake loaded with butter and sugar. It was a nutritional bread that was common during Bible days. Verse 7 says: *"And the angel of the Lord came again the second time, and touched him, and said, Arise and eat; because the journey is too great for thee."*

My brothers and sisters, you cannot eat chocolate ice cream for breakfast, barbecue potato chips for lunch, and pepperoni pizza for dinner, and then think you are physically and mentally healthy. You have to eat nutritious food. Sometimes when I visit people in the hospital, I find that they are not eating their food. They say they don't want it because they don't like the way it tastes. I tell them, "The food is not for you; it's for your body."

Pay close attention to what happened in verse 8: *"And he arose, and did eat and drink, and went in the strength of that meat forty days and forty nights unto Horeb the mount of God."* After eating bread and drinking water to gain his strength, Elijah fasted forty days and nights during his three hundred mile journey to Mount Horeb. It was a long, difficult trip through the desert. He finally arrived near the mountain of Sinai, the same place where Moses received the Ten Commandments. As a result of Elijah's fast, God revealed Himself in a new way, in a new place.

If you are in a state of depression like Elijah, you must find a place where you can be alone with God. It can be in your own home. Just go to a secret place, shut the door, turn off the telephone and television, tell your friends you will see them later, and talk to God. Many times, God won't speak to you in a crowd. You need to be alone to hear Him. You need to be alone so you can find strength in studying His Word.

Sometimes when I am driving to my hometown of Columbus, Texas, I go around the back way where the leaves on the trees are blowing in the wind and the cows are grazing in the grass. I know I can get there faster driving on the interstate, but sometimes I need the peace and quiet. Find a place to be alone with God regularly. It is not enough to be with Him at eleven o'clock on Sunday.

In I Kings 19:9, God speaks to Elijah: *"And he came thither unto a cave, and lodged there; and, behold, the word of the Lord came to him, and he said unto him, What doest thou here, Elijah?"* Elijah started telling the Lord about how hard he had been working, how people were trying to kill him, and how he was the only one left who served Him. Sometimes when we are down, we think we are the only one who is right. I have seen people who find Jesus on Sunday and are calling everyone else a sinner on Monday. We want to impress God, but God says, "So what?"

Look at what God told Elijah in verses 11–12:

> *And he said, Go forth, and stand upon the mount before the Lord. And, behold, the Lord passed by, and a great and strong wind rent the mountains, and brake in pieces the rocks before the Lord; but the Lord was not in the wind: and after the wind an earthquake; but the Lord was not in the earthquake: And after the earthquake a fire; but the Lord was not in the fire.*

No doubt, Elijah thought the wind was God, but the Lord was not in the wind. After the wind, there was an earthquake. But the Lord was not in the earthquake. After the earthquake, a fire came, but the Lord was not in the fire. Then, at the end, there came *"a still small voice."*

God speaks in a still, small voice. God used the earthquake, wind, and fire to shake Elijah to his senses. God is not going to talk to you while you are making a lot of noise; nor is He going to play hide and seek with you. If you be still and settle down, then God will help you. When He gets your attention, then He will speak in a still, small voice.

Until God delivered me, I suffered with asthma. When I went to the hospital because of an asthma attack, they would tell me to calm down and breathe slowly. This is what God is telling us today. He wants us to settle down so he can speak to us.

At this point, Elijah was still depressed. If you look at verse 13, you will see that God asks again, "Why are you here Elijah?" Elijah told God the same thing again. He went on about how he had served him zealously, and that the Israelites were killing all the prophets. God told Elijah to go to Damascus and anoint a new king over Syria, and then anoint a new king over Israel to replace Ahab. Then, God told Elijah that he was wrong in thinking that he was the only one in Israel true to Him. There were still seven thousand who did not worship Baal. Elijah was encouraged to know that there were others who were true to God, and left Sinai on another long journey.

When you are going through turmoil, get up and do something to get out of your situation. Get out of bed, take a bath, put on some clean clothes, and comb your hair. Get out of the house and go for a walk.

Spend some time alone with the Lord. Then, when the Lord brings you out of the depths of depression, thank Him, and tell yourself that you are not going back. God is our refuge and strength, a very present help in trouble. There is no need for you to ever go back.

DO YOU NEED A BREAKTHROUGH?

Here are some additional words of advice that will help you break the yoke of depression through fasting and praying:

- Feeling blue can be like a bad habit that you get comfortable with. We all have things in our lives we aren't happy with. They can get better or worse depending on how we deal with them. Work on developing good habits, like finding peace in prayer.

- If you are unable to fast due to medical reasons, remember you can always pray. And you can talk to God anytime, any place. First Thessalonians 5:17 says, *"Pray without ceasing."* Philippians 4:6 says: *"Be careful for nothing; but in every thing by prayer and supplication with thanksgiving let your requests be made known unto God."* In other words, don't worry about anything, but pray about everything.

- Never be afraid or ashamed to seek mental health care. If you break your arm, you see a doctor. If you have problems with your eyes, you see an ophthalmologist. If you have a toothache, you see a dentist. So by all means, seek professional help, if there is something troubling your mind.

Fasting and Praying for Patience

T here are times in life when we all must wait on answers from God. Waiting, however, is one of the hardest things in the world for us to do. That is when we need patience, and one way to obtain patience is through fasting and praying. When you fast and pray, you refresh yourself spiritually and combat the chaos that is present in so many of our lives. We become better at operating on God's time, not our time.

God laid this message of patience on my heart during a time when I needed it most. We were two or three weeks away from the completion of our second church, and God had to slow me down. One of the Scriptures He gave me was Galatians 6:9, which says, *"And let us not be weary in well doing: for in due season we shall reap, if we faint not."* Notice that it does not say *your* season, but *due* season. Am I making sense?

Many of us have already prayed to God about something, and we are looking for an answer. One thing we should know about prayer is that God does not always answer with a "Yes." And He does not always answer with a "No." Sometimes, God says, "Wait." But it is hard for us to wait patiently on the Lord, especially since we live in a society where we have to have everything now. We want to know when, and we want to know right now. Don't tell me, I'll know later. I don't want to hear about "By and by, when the morning comes." I want to know now!

I like to say that we have developed a microwave mentality. Those of us who remember when microwaves were not around had to wait a long time for our potatoes to bake, our frozen dinners to cook, or our meat to thaw. Now, look at us! An hour of cooking time has been reduced to minutes, yet we stand in front of the microwave about to have a fit because our popcorn is taking too long to pop or the cheese on our pizza is taking too long to melt.

We thank God for instant potatoes because we don't have to peel them anymore. We thank God for instant credit because we don't have to wait long for approval. We thank God for pushbutton phones because those rotary phones took too long to dial a number.

Recently, I went to a store where you had to take a number and wait your turn to receive service. My number was fifty-eight. When I looked up at the monitor, they were serving number forty-five. I stood there waiting and told myself, "Reverend, you need to be patient." Then it took them ten minutes to get to number forty-six. I waited for them to go a little further, but it was taking so long that I decided to come back later. Just as I got ready to leave, someone came up to me and said, "Reverend Booker, I listened to you last Sunday on television. I really enjoyed your message. It was on patience." I went ahead and waited because Reverend needed to practice what he preached. I learned to have patience right there.

God wants us to learn to wait on Him. It may seem as if your dreams will never come true, but that's because God has put us in a spiritual growth process. For us, it is often a slow process because we want an answer now. We believe that if we pray, attend Bible study, and become good Christians, the Lord will hurry up. But you cannot hurry God, you just have to wait.

Still, we wonder why a Christian puts his house on the market and it takes a year for it to sell while a sinner puts his house on the market and it sells in a month. We wonder why we pay our tithes and still have financial problems while someone who never gives God a dime seems to prosper. I do not have all the answers, but I do know that God carries us through struggles until we are ready to handle what

He has for us. Sometimes, storms are better for us than sunshine because they make us realize who God is.

One Bible story that illustrates the importance of patience is the story of Lazarus in John 11. Verse 1 begins, *"Now a certain man was sick, named Lazarus, of Bethany, the town of Mary and her sister Martha."* In verse 2, we are reminded that it was Mary who anointed the Lord with ointment and wiped his feet with her hair. Because Lazarus was ill, his sisters, Mary and Martha, sent a note to Jesus saying, *"Lord, behold, he whom thou lovest is sick" (John 11:3).*

Some things in a letter are not written. They appear between the lines, and you have to look closely to find them. What the sisters meant was that Jesus needed to drop what He was doing and come see about Lazarus because He loved him. They were saying that when Jesus came to Bethany, they gave Him a place to lay His head. When He was hungry, they fed Him.

We are the same way. We think Jesus should drop everything and help us just because we go to church. We think Jesus should turn a flip because we love Him, but Jesus doesn't operate like that. Jesus received the message from Mary and Martha, but He stayed in the where He was for two days. On the third day, when He was ready, verses 7–8 tell us:

Then after that saith he to his disciples, Let us go into Judea again. His disciples saith unto him, Master, the Jews of late sought to stone thee; and goest thou thither again?

Put yourself in the disciples' place. They were going to a dangerous place, and they could not handle it. Just like us sometimes, they did not believe God could handle it. But God can do anything. Jesus told them they were going anyway. He said that there are twelve hours in a day. He was the Son of God, the Light of the world, and when they walked with Him, they were protected. But if they walked in the night, they would stumble because the devil would have a "field day."

John 11:11 says, *"These things said he: and after that he saith unto them, Our friend Lazarus sleepeth; but I go, that I may awake him out of sleep."* In verse 12, the disciples wanted to know why Jesus was going to wake him up because sick folk need rest. They were talking about sleep, and Jesus was talking about death. If you know the Lord and you are dead, all you are doing is sleeping.

Look at verse 16: *"Then said Thomas, which is called Didymus, unto his fellow disciples, Let us also go, that we may die with him."* The word *Didymus* means "twin." All of us have a twin in us. We say one thing, but our twin says something else. If we say, "I know the Lord will make a way somehow," the twin says, "Don't you believe it." Some of us need to look in the mirror and ask ourselves, "Who's talking?" When the storms roll in and all hell still breaks loose, although you have done the best you can, what does your twin say then?

Although Thomas walked with Jesus, and saw the work that He did, he still thought they were going to die with Him. Some of us have forgotten how good God has been to us, and how many times He has brought us out of trouble. I believe there are some Brother and Sister Thomases walking around. You have your face full of faith, but God can see the doubt in your heart.

GOD'S TIME

When Jesus got to Bethany, Lazarus had been in the grave for four days. Verses 20–23 read:

> *Then Martha, as soon as she heard that Jesus was coming, went and met him: but Mary sat still in the house. Then said Martha unto Jesus, Lord, if thou hadst been here, my brother had not died. But I know, that even now, whatsoever though wilt ask of God, God will give it thee. Jesus saith unto her, Thy brother shall rise again.*

Can you see where Martha was short on patience? She told Jesus that since He did not come when they called Him, they had to wait. But if He had been there,

Lazarus would not have died. But then in verse 22, she caught herself and said that she knew whatever Jesus asked God for, God would grant it. Jesus heard all of that and, in verse 23, told her that her brother would be alright.

How many of us have told God it was too late, but then the Holy Spirit came in and said, "It is never too late?" If that has happened to you, then you ought to tell the Lord, "Excuse me for doubting you." Sometimes we really have to look back and remember who Jesus is. He is the resurrection. In verse 27, Martha said, *"Yea, Lord: I believe that thou art the Christ, the Son of God, which should come into the world."* Martha had to remember who Jesus was.

In verse 34, Jesus asked where had they lain Lazarus. They told Him to *"come see."* Verse 35 says simply, *"Jesus wept."*

When Jesus arrived at the cave where Lazarus was buried, He told them to take away the stone. God blesses us, but He often wants us to participate in the blessing. Jesus wanted them to take away the stone of doubt. Martha could not understand why Jesus wanted the stone taken away because Lazarus had been dead for four days, and by this time he was stinking. Jesus did not ask Martha how Lazarus smelled; He said take away the stone. If Lazarus was stinking, it meant that he was dead, and it would take more than a man to bring him back to life. You see, God is always on time, and what is late for us is an opportunity for God. When we give up, that is just the right time for God to step in. God shines best in our darkest hour.

Again, I remember the construction of our second location. I carried those blueprints around for three years until God got ready to build that building. It was three years until God said, "It's time."

Are you waiting for a breakthrough today? Is your marriage crumbling? Is your house about to fall apart? Are you ready to give up on your children? I want to let you know that it is never too late for God. He will take away the stone.

In verses 41–43, they moved the stone, Jesus thanked God for hearing Him, and then He went into the grave and cried in a loud voice, *"Lazarus, come forth!"* I liken it to when I was growing up, and my mother finished cooking. She would call, "Ya'll come!" and everybody would make a beeline to the table. Sometimes Mother would cook something special for me, and she would say, "Junior." She wasn't calling my other brothers and sisters, she was calling me.

Jesus called Lazarus by his name, but he wasn't through yet. The Jewish custom was to wrap the dead in grave clothes and tie their hands and feet. Jesus told them to loose Lazarus by taking off his grave clothes so he would be free. God wants to bless us—loose us—but we still have on our grave clothes. I used to hear my mother walk around and say, "Loose, devil." I believe we need to tell the devil, "You're a liar! You're not going to bind me because God has given me the victory." Tell Satan to get out of your way, loose you and let you go.

Just as Jesus performed a miracle by raising Lazarus from the dead, He can perform miracles in our lives. All we have to do is trust Him, and believe that He is always on time.

DO YOU NEED A BREAKTHROUGH?

I would like to leave you with the following Scriptures to meditate on when you are fasting and praying for patience:

> **Wait** on the Lord; be of good courage, and he shall strengthen thine heart; **wait**, I say, on the Lord (Psalm 27:14).

> But they that **wait** upon the Lord shall renew their strength; they shall mount up with wings as eagles; they shall run, and not be weary; and they shall walk, and not faint (Isaiah 40:31).

*For whatsoever things were written aforetime were written for our learning, that we through **patience** and comfort of the scriptures might have hope (Romans 15:4).*

*That ye be not slothful, but followers of them who through faith and **patience** inherit the promises (Hebrews 6:12).*

*Knowing this, that the trying of your faith worketh **patience**. But let **patience** have her perfect work, that ye may be perfect and entire, wanting nothing (James 1:3–4).*

*Be ye also **patient**; stablish your hearts: for the coming of the Lord draweth nigh (James 5:8).*

My Fasting Journal

The following pages are provided to encourage you to begin fasting on a regular basis. Use these pages to record your fasting experiences. There is space for you to record the date, what you prayed, and the Scriptures you based your prayer on. When God answers, record the date and the answer He gave you. Be sure to thank God for every answer, even if He says, "No" or "Wait."

Later, when you review these pages, you will be able to see the powerful hand of God at work in your life and your spiritual growth.

After getting started here, I recommend creating a journal to record your prayers and God's answers as you continue practicing the discipline of fasting and praying. May God bless you greatly!

Date:

My Prayer Request:

Scripture(s):

God's Answer:

Date:

My Prayer Request:

Scripture(s):

God's Answer:

Date:

My Prayer Request:

Scripture(s):

God's Answer:

Date:

My Prayer Request:

Scripture(s):

God's Answer:

Date:

My Prayer Request:

Scripture(s):

God's Answer:

Date:

My Prayer Request:

Scripture(s):

God's Answer:

Date:

My Prayer Request:

Scripture(s):

God's Answer:

About the Author

Reverend Gusta Booker is the senior pastor of Greater St. Matthew Church in Houston, Texas. Greater St. Matthew is one church with two locations, and is one of the fastest growing churches in Houston. Pastor Booker's television and radio ministries can be seen and heard in Houston, Austin, and Beaumont.

Pastor Booker began Greater St. Matthew in 1968 with eight charter members who met in his home for six months. In 1969, the congregation moved to a ninety-seat sanctuary on Jutland Road. The congregation continued to grow, and the church was enlarged in the 1970s and 1980s. In 1994, the church opened a Southwest location for worship services. A thirty thousand square feet multi-ministry complex was completed in 2001 that includes a two thousand-seat sanctuary, family life center and academy.

Pastor Booker is an author, Bible scholar, educator and religious leader. In addition to *Making Sense of*

Fasting and Praying, he has written two other books: *After the Honeymoon* and *Living Beyond the Pain.*

He is the founder and first moderator of the Gulf Coast Baptist Association, past president of the Central Baptist State Convention of Texas, and chairman of the Christian Education Board of the National Baptist Convention of America. He is presently secretary/ treasurer of the Media Board of the National Baptist Convention. In July 2004, Pastor Booker was inducted into to the Religious Hall of Fame in Dallas, Texas.

A native of Columbus, Texas, Pastor Booker is the youngest of nine children born to the late Rev. Gusta Booker, Sr. and the late Mrs. Gussie Booker. He received a bachelor's degree in education from Texas Southern University and a master's degree in theology from Inter-Baptist Theological Seminary. He is a former dean of Southside Theological Seminary and a former teacher in Houston public schools.

Pastor Booker is happily married to Theola Massie Booker. They have three children—Ronald, Gusta III, and Alita Corine—and two daughters-in-law, Valree and Nicole. They also have three grandchildren— Ronald Jr., Joshua, and Peyton Nicole Booker.